A STRAIGHTFORWARD GUIDE
TO
SETTING UP YOUR OWN
BUSINESS

LIAM YOUNG

Straightforward Publishing Limited
38 Cromwell Road, London E17 9JN

© Straightforward Publishing
First Edition 1996

British Library Cataloguing in Publication data.
A Catalogue record for this book is available
from the British Library.

ISBN   1 8 99924 45 0

Printed by BPC Wheaton - Exeter

Cover Design by Straightforward Graphics

Whilst every effort has been taken to ensure the
information given in this book is accurate at the
time the book was printed, the author and
publishers recognise that information can become
out of date. The book is therefore sold on the
condition that no responsibility for errors or
omissions is assumed. The authors and publishers
cannot be held liable for any loss which is a
result of the use of any information contained
herein.

CONTENTS

Introduction

INTRODUCTION

Starting a business is a significant step and if you wish to succeed, and not become one of the numerous casualties, then it is of the utmost importance that you understand the requirements of starting your own business and have a clear idea of what it is you are selling. What is your product and who wants or needs it? Without a clear idea of the nature of your business you will probably fail, notwithstanding the fact that the idea was good.

Small business plays a vital part in the economy, both in creating jobs and also providing competition and innovation. For a small business to succeed, the entrepreneurs running the business will have a clear idea of their product, unique selling points, marketing, finance, pricing, type of premises needed to operate from and keeping books and accounts. Underpinning this will be the business plan.

This book will take you through each of these areas and will give you a clear idea of what is required to start your business and the responsibilities involved. The world needs entrepreneurs, the economy needs entrepreneurs and innovation. However, your business will only be vital if you plan its creation successfully.

Good Luck!

1.
DEVELOPING YOUR BUSINESS IDEA

There are a number of steps involved in developing your business idea, developing it to the point of being in control of a viable business. This book will take you through those steps. However, the very first step is to find a product to manufacture, a service to offer, or an idea for one. Although your choice will partly depend on your skills and interests, it must also provide what customers are looking for. Without the sales of your product your business is not viable.

Try and choose something that you have an interest in, that you enjoy selling and that there is a demand for. Most ideas are not original. Therefore, when you look at an idea you need to think about how you will differentiate your product from others. In marketing terms this is called "branding" or creating your own unique image.

Examining the market

Before you decide on your product, or decide on a way to earn a living, take a close look at the needs and demands of the marketplace. Be led by the market and not only by what you want to do. This book will deal with marketing in some depth later on. We will also be looking at pricing of products, which you must understand and get right if you are to succeed.

Levels of Investment in your business

Businesses start with varying amounts of capital. Some start with minimum outlay others require vast amounts to bring them into being. It is unlikely that anyone reading this book will fall into the latter category. However, it is crucial that you estimate the level of initial investment that you will need to make in the early stages of your business and also what your cashflow will be in the future. This book will address sources of finance and also will discuss the type and nature of the business plan required for your business in the early stages.

Your skills and your Ideas

If you are considering starting a business which is a totally different area to your work, and which requires skills which are somewhat different, it may be wise to continue with your current job and absorb the new skills needed and re-orientate yourself to the new culture first. New skills take a while to gain and you are advised to be cautious in the first instance.

If you lack the basic skills to help you make the transition to a new area of work then you should consider specific training. There are plenty of

3

courses around. You should ask at your local training and enterprise council.

Different business Ideas

Small markets

There are numerous small markets that larger companies are uninterested in. They may have rationalized their business to such an extent that they are no longer interested in smaller areas, or segments. Larger companies find it difficult to react quickly to frequent variations in demand and taste.

The new small business should identify these markets and exploit them. This is essential to achieving growth and future success.

The retail market

If you are considering retailing then you will always require an investment of capital in order to obtain premises, whether buying or leasing. You will also need some managerial skills. However, there are certain retail outlets that are easier to succeed in than others, for a number of reasons. When considering retailing, you should take into account the following:

some shops require you to work long hours, for example, newsagents,

4

tobacconists and florists. Other shops will require you to stock a large range of diverse products, i.e. gift shops, jewellery shops etc.

There are businesses which will require you to employ highly trained staff, i.e. antiques, photography etc. This can have implications for your salary bill, unless you intend to run the business yourself. Other business will require you to provide a good after sales service, such as the provision of appliances.

Whatever area you decide to operate in, you should always think through the implications of entering into a specific area. This is where the business plan will help you. We will be discussing the business plan later.

Franchising

Operating a franchise removes some of the initial risks involved in setting up a business. This is because you will be selling a product which is tried and tested and already has had the benefit of strong marketing. We will be discussing franchises later on in the book. You can contact the British Franchise Association if you require further advice (see useful addresses at the back of the book).

Import and export businesses

Importing could enable you to provide a product that is cheaper than those produced at home. This is because many home markets have collapsed because of competition from abroad. However, you need to research your market thoroughly and be confident that you understand the business culture of the countries that you are dealing with. Many people have lost money abroad because they have become the victim of unscrupulous businessmen. The Embassy relating to the country you will deal with will be able to give you advice and assistance and will alert you to some of the pitfalls.

Export too has become a lot more significant since the single European market was declared open for business in 1993. There is now a single market of over 300 million potential customers with routine clearance of commercial goods. Although these changes have made trading in Europe easier there are still significant differences in the way goods and services are presented to different nationalities and also in business practice and style.

Foreign languages have never been a strong point of British people and therefore, if you intend to develop an export business, you may well be advised to brush up on European languages. If potential customers feel that you are making the effort then this will probably lead to more effective business relations. The Department of Trade and Industry is very active in promoting trade in Europe, and elsewhere. They have issued a publication called "Business in Europe" which offers practical advice to help businesses compete successfully in Europe.

If you are thinking of expanding into Europe then you will need to get information on VAT, market research and consumer tastes, plus many other areas. Your local Training and Enterprise Council office should put you in touch with local networks.

Using Matching Agencies

If you have some money but are uncertain about the type of business you wish to start, it is a good idea to contact a matching agency which will find a suitable business idea for you. If you have a good idea, but not enough capital or experience to develop it you should try contacting Venture Capital Report Limited and the Local Investment Networking Company (see useful addresses)

Selling products and services

People with experience in selling can try contacting the Manufacturers Agents Association and the British Agents Register (see useful addresses).These organizations will put you in touch with manufacturers and suppliers who cannot afford to employ a permanent sales force of their own and may be interested in taking on a freelance representative. Other manufacturers may be dealing with a very fragmented market and it might be more cost effective for them to place their goods with representatives who are carrying more than one line.

Manufacturing

If you have capital and the right skills it is possible to run a small manufacturing firm profitably. However you will need to have sufficient spare, or risk, capital to invest in buildings, machines, tools and raw materials.

You will also need to know about marketing, sales, distribution, financial control and managing people. If you have thought up an original idea but you don't want to deal with the whole business yourself, you might be able to find a business to take on certain aspects (e.g. invoicing and distribution) Another option is to try and find someone with whom you can pool resources-perhaps sharing office space or secretarial help. Do remember to protect any new ideas before telling any interested party about it. Many people have found their idea "pirated" by unscrupulous others.

Providing services

This is a growth area and you should investigate it thoroughly before entering into it. You should remember that people experience services and you need to concentrate on how you can make your product concrete and tangible. It is possible to start a service business with only a small outlay of capital and with very little risk of losing your money. However, many of the opportunities may be local and your success will

8

very much depend on what is already available. This is where careful market research comes in.

Some examples of services that you could provide are business services, e.g. typing, computing, word processing, office cleaning and recruitment. Publishing and writing services are popular but can be difficult to sustain because of the nature of cashflow in the business. However, editorial services, proof reading and copy writing can be lucrative.

Home services, such as gardening, plumbing and general building, property management and window cleaning are viable services to offer, requiring little capital initially. However, some experience will be needed of certain areas, in particular property management.

Professional services are potentially lucrative, such as dentistry, business management and consultancy, plus marketing and research. However, again you will need specific skills to embark on these specific ventures. Personal services such as massage, counselling, stress therapy and psychotherapy are growth areas but will require skills in those specific areas.

Catering

Catering can be lucrative and often has the advantage of being a cash business, as opposed to a business where you will wait weeks and months to get paid. Such businesses include running your own take away food outlet, café or restaurant and providing meals for offices. Sandwich bars are popular, require little capital in the first instance and are cash generators. Catering for parties can also be lucrative.

Above are only a few ideas for business. However, it does raise awareness to the fact that you should always consider carefully the area which you have chosen. Make sure that you have done your research and you know your product. You must be single minded when creating a business, passionate about your product and determined to succeed.

10

2 The Service and the Product generally

In Chapter one, we discussed business ideas generally. In this chapter we will move forward a step and address the initial stages of planning crucial to setting up your own business.

When planning and developing your business idea 3 fundamental questions need to be addressed:

* What is the nature of the business that you are entering into?

* What is it about you that makes you a competent business person both generally and also in relation to your particular business?

* What is it that makes your particular product or service   special? What is your unique selling point (usp)?

Business description-service and product

At first, describing your business in detail might seem like entering into irrelevant detail, after all, a butchers a butcher and an architects an architect... or are they? Take the butcher. The butcher could have   any

11

one of a number of usp's, including the following:

- specialist in continental meats and sausages

- catering for certain ethnic/religious groups (halal, kosher)

- provider of non factory farmed products

_ provider of certain ready made dishes, e.g., specially marinaded chops for barbecues, skewer kebabs etc

- provider of home delivery service

- employment of highly trained, qualified staff, able to give advice on both products and food preparation.

- lower cost than competitors

- provision of delicatessen services

- particularly convenient location

It is important to consider very carefully about what exactly it is you are proposing to sell because in so doing you are forced to think about your "competitive edge", your USP. The consequence of not having a competitive edge is, quite simply, failure. If it is not failure, then it

12

means that you are operating a monopoly, or entering into a market in which demand outstrips supply. Even then, it is crucial to remember that the market or excess demand should not last forever.

Let us think about an architect. An architects unique selling point could be that he or she:

- is particularly highly qualified or experienced in their job, with an excellent track record and a long list of clients

- specialises in certain types of design, e.g., adapted rooms for people with disabilities

- caters for a particular client or set of clients, e.g., public sector landlords

- provides other, related services (e.g. surveying, quantity surveying etc)

Consequently, in describing your business you inevitably have to address the issue of USP.

Exercise 1

Draw up a list of possible unique selling points for the following businesses:

13

* a bookshop

* a clothes manufacturer

* a cinema

* a solicitors practice

* a public house

You as a business person

Have you got what it takes to be a successful business manager? Do you have the necessary skills, qualifications and experience to enable you to be successful in the field of business that you have chosen? When planning the setting up of a business, you will be formulating a business plan along the way. Any good business plan will contain within it a C.V. of all of the key staff involved in the business. Not surprisingly, it will contain a particularly detailed C.V. of the person-or persons-responsible for running the business, the managers.

At this point, it is important to bear in mind the fact that the business plan can be, and usually is, a marketing document-that is, a document that will be read by possible funders and, in some cases, clients. Therefore, exactly how you word and present the C.V. needs to be taken into consideration.

14

The C.V. should include certain personal details relating to the managers or owners (if different) of the business, including name, address and date of birth. The reasons for giving name and address are obvious: no one is going to want to do business with an anonymous client. Date of birth is usually something that may not be of interest to some readers of the C.V. However, a bank manager would want to know if it was viable to lend money to someone whose age suggests that they might not be in business long enough to pay back any loan that they take out, or whether the owner of the business is likely to be sufficiently mature as to handle well the responsibilities of a business person.

The above information constitutes formal detail, and it should come at the start of a business plan, preceding the business description. It is in describing the skills, qualifications and experience of the staff, especially the owners and managers, that a business plan explains how the proposed business is to be viable in terms of personnel.

What are the particular skills, qualifications and experience that are required to run any business successfully?

A successful business person will have skills/qualifications/experience in relation to all of the following, albeit in varying proportions:

- personnel management (especially important if employing staff)

- financial management

15

- initiative, dynamism, imagination

- leadership

- social skills

If the C.V. of the manager successfully demonstrates the above, then the business plan goes a long way towards convincing the reader that the author of the plan is a serious business person.

If employing staff, the author should highlight any experience that they have had in supervising staff. Such experience might have been gained in previous employment, e.g., as a shop manager. Alternatively, it may have been gained in a voluntary capacity (e.g., as a management committee member of a local charity).

It might also be demonstrated by reference to relevant professional qualifications. In addition, if the author cannot legitimately refer to any of the above, he or she can draw upon comparable experience of supervising people in a formal capacity, perhaps as a teacher or nursery nurse. Finally, if this is not too feasible then it is possible to demonstrate personnel management by reference to informal experience of supervising people.

Similar to the above, there are numerous ways of demonstrating financial management skills. For example, it is possible to point to previous employment experience as an accountant, a book keeper etc.

16

On the other hand, you may have a professional qualification in finance or you may have gained experience in a voluntary capacity. Lastly, you can always draw upon your informal experience of budget management, either through the family or some other capacity.

Having considered your business and the skills and talents of those people who will run it, it is necessary to take the next step in setting up your business, that is the consideration of the structure of your business. There are a number of ways of setting up your business, from sole trader to partnership to limited company. It is vital that you understand the various structures that your business can operate within and that you have chosen the right one.

17

3 THE STRUCTURE OF YOUR BUSINESS

There are various structures within which your business can operate and it is essential that you understand the nature of each structure.

THE SOLE, OR PROPRIETARY, BUSINESS

This is a business owned by one person. If you are operating alone then this may be suitable for your purposes. The person and the business are legally one and the same. It does not matter what or who you trade as, the business is inseparable from yourself, as opposed to a limited company, which is a separate entity.

All financial risk is taken by that one person and all that persons assets are included in that risk. The one big advantage is that all decisions can be taken by the one person without interference.

A second advantage is that the administrative costs of running a sole business are small, if your business is VAT registered then you will need to keep records, as you will for the inland revenue. However, there are no other legal requirements.

Partnerships

Partnership is a business where two or more people are joined by an agreement to run that business together. The agreement is usually written, given the potential pitfalls that can arise from a partnership.

Liabilities which may arise are shared jointly and severally and this should be made clear to anyone entering a partnership. Even if you only have 1% of the business you will still be responsible for 100% of the liability. All personal assets of each partner are at risk if the business fails.

Decisions are taken jointly, as laid down by the partnership agreement. If the agreement lays down that partners have differing decision making capacity dependent upon their shareholding then it could be that, in a three way partnership, the decision making process may be hampered because a decision cannot be reached unless the major investor is present.

It is very important indeed to consider the nature of the agreement that you are entering into and it may also be advisable to take legal advice.

Partnership usually reflects the way that business was capitalised although other factors may be taken into consideration. For example, an expert in a particular field may join with an investor to create a 50/50 partnership.

19

It is very advisable indeed to consider carefully the ramifications of entering into a partnership. Many such arrangements end in tears, with both partners hostile to each other. Personal bankruptcy can occur as can the ruin of the partner(s).

Profits are usually shared between partners in accordance with the terms in the agreement.

THE LIMITED LIABILITY COMPANY

This type of company has evolved over the years and provides a framework within which a business can operate effectively. A limited company is usually the best vehicle for business, in all but the smallest of business. It is certainly the only sensible answer if capital is being introduced by those who are not actively involved in running the business (shareholders).

Shareholders inject capital and receive a return (dividend) in proportion to the capital they invest. They are eligible to attend an annual general meeting to approve or otherwise the way the directors are running the business. Annual General meetings also determine how much of the profit will be distributed to shareholders.

Voting is in accordance with the number of shares held and the meeting can replace all or any of the directors if a majority are dissatisfied with them.

20

Shareholders can, if a majority request, call an Extraordinary General Meeting to question directors about performance, outside the Cycle of Annual General Meetings.

Control of the company is in the hands of directors who are appointed by the shareholders to run the company on their behalf.

The company is a legal entity in its own right and stands alone from the directors and shareholders, who have limited liability.

When a company is created it will have an "Authorised Shareholding" that specifies the limit of a shareholders liability. If all shares have been issued then shareholders are not liable for any more debts that the company may accrue.

THE FRANCHISE

Franchising is just one word to describe a number of varying business relationships-some big, some small, some complex. Essentially, a properly constructed franchise involves a well established company offering an individual the opportunity to trade under its corporate name. The company will also provide well proven know how, a marketing programme, training, research and development facilities and, often, bulk buying and administrative facilities.

The individual, in return, pays for the privilege-usually by way of an

21

initial fee, followed by a continuing levy, most often expressed as a percentage of sales.

The British Franchise Association, 75A Bell Street, Henley on Thames, Oxfordshire RG9 2BD will advise you on the various pitfalls and can point you in the right direction. From them, you can purchase a "Franchisee pack" which contains some useful hints on being a franchisee and also includes an up to date list of those companies which are members of the Association.

It is essential, when considering forming a company, that you have a clear idea of what type of structure should relate to your business. If you need further advice concerning business structure, you should contact the Department of Trade and Industry, whose address is at the rear of this book.

PATENTS, REGISTERED DESIGNS, SERVICE MARKS AND COPYRIGHT

In order to grow, industry must continually create and develop new ideas. Innovation is expensive and innovators need protection, to ensure that others cannot pirate their ideas. All of the above items are known as "intellectual property" and, with the exception of copyright, in order to register and protect your intellectual property, you need to contact the patent office. Their address can be obtained from the Chartered Institute of Patent Agents, whose number is at the rear of this book.

22

PATENT

If you or your company have produced what you consider is a unique product or process, it is very important to register it as soon as possible, before disclosing it to anyone. The granting of a patent gives the patentee a monopoly to make, use or sell an invention for a fixed period of time. This is currently a maximum of twenty years.

REGISTERED DESIGNS

This involves registering what you consider to be a new design. The proprietor must register before offering for sale in the U.K. the new design.

A trademark is a means of identification-whether a word or a logo-which is used in the course of trade in order to identify and distinguish to the purchaser that the goods in question are yours. A good trademark is a very important marketing aid and you are strongly advised to register it.

SERVICE MARKS

This register extends the trademark to cover not only goods but also services. If you are running a hotel for example, you can now register your service mark if you have one.

COPYRIGHT

Unlike the other four categories, copyright is established by evidence of creation, and protection is automatic. To safeguard your position, it might be sensible to deposit your work with your bank or your solicitor or send a copy of your work to yourself by registered post.

It should be noted that there is no copyright attached to a name or title, only the work itself.

Having given thought to the likely structure of your business, we need now to consider, in Chapter four, the right location for your business and also questions relating to the employment and management of staff.

4 LOCATION OF YOUR BUSINESS. MANAGING STAFF

Location of your business

To be within easy reach of your customers may be vital or it may be totally unimportant. If you have a retail business, location is a major consideration. If you are in mail order, you can operate from anywhere in the country so far as your customers are concerned. If you are a wholesaler, do you require a showroom? If you are operating a factory, do you anticipate the requirement for a factory shop? is it simply a question of being conveniently located for your customers or are you relying on passing trade? It is vital that, in assessing the right location, you first clearly define the extent to which you need to make yourself accessible to your customers.

In an ideal world, you should be looking to acquire the right accommodation for your scale of operation today and for your expansion plans this year, next year and some years in the future. This applies whether you are looking for a shop, an office, a workshop or a factory unit. Before you start looking for new premises, work out carefully just what it is you need now.

The Important questions to consider are:

How many square feet of offices/storage space/workshop/showroom?

How many square feet of employees facilities?

How much car parking space?

How much outside storage for deliveries, storage and packing?

If you are uncertain as to what precisely you need, or you feel that the shape of your business is going to alter substantially and in the short term, do not commit yourself to a hefty purchase, or even as much as a five year lease. Go instead for a temporary solution, while you determine what your long term requirements are likely to be.

Never enter into a lengthy commitment unless you feel that the premises are likely to suit you in the long term. Whether you are buying a freehold or acquiring a lease, take independent professional advice as to the value. Hire a surveyor who will tell you whether the asking price or rent is fair. Whatever your business, the cost of your premises is going to represent a major overhead. If you get it wrong, you will go out of business.

It is essential to establish that not only can the property be used for the purpose for which you want it, but also that the planning consent will cover any future business development.

26

Working from home

Particularly if you are starting a new business, the idea of working from home is attractive. It enables you to keep your overheads to a minimum, allows you to work the long hours necessary in the establishment of a business, and leaves your options open. If the business does not work out, you are not committed to an industrial property. It needs to be recognized, however, that working from home can cause considerable problems.

Strictly speaking, if you plan to run a business from home, almost certainly you will need approval or permission either from someone or some authority. There are two kinds of restrictions which may affect your ability to run your business from home. The first is a series of contractual relationships which you may have already entered into, such as a tenancy or lease. The second is that imposed by local authorities-planning, highways health and safety.

Planning permission

If you want to make a significant alteration to your house in order to accommodate your business, you will need planning permission or building regulations approval. This includes building an extension, loft conversion, in fact almost anything except extremely simple alterations.

Change of use

Local authorities state that consent has to be sought for any change of use. The interpretation of change of use is difficult but what you have to decide is whether what you wish to do constitutes a genuine material change of use of the building.

You should make sure that you have insurance to cover your business activity within your home. If you have an accident which occurs as a direct result of your business then your insurance will not cover it.

Inspectors

There are two types of inspector-local authority inspectors and fire authority inspectors. Local Authority inspectors are concerned with premises where the main activities are:

The sale or storage of goods for retail or wholesale distribution.

Office activities

Catering Services

Provision of residential accommodation

Consumer services provided in shop premises

Dry Cleaning in coin operated units in launderettes

The keeping of wild animals for exhibition to the public

Fire Authority Inspectors

The fire authority requires that a place of work should have a fire certificate, and in order for your business to get a fire certificate, the premises need to be inspected. The fire authority will wish to see that there is adequate provision for a means of escape in case of fire, and the necessary amount of equipment. The Fire inspectors will advise you these facilities are inadequate, tell you how they can be put right and then re-inspect the premises when you have carried out the necessary work.

Employing People

At first you may be able to run your business by yourself or with help from your family. But if not, as your business expands, you may need to employ people. Before doing this, some businesses may consider it worthwhile subcontracting work. This may be more cost effective in ironing out short term trading highs and lows. However, if you do need to take on employees, then you must do certain things.

What are my responsibilities as an employer?

You must give every employee a written statement of terms of

29

employment. At the time of publication, by law, all employees working 16 or more hours a week must be given a written statement of terms after they have worked 13 weeks in the job.

This statement must include the following:

* name of employer

* name of employee, job title and description

* hours of work

* pay details, including how often the employee is paid

* holidays

* grievance procedures

* sickness and injury procedures

* pension schemes

* length of notice needed to end employment

* disciplinary rules, including dress and behaviour

30

Discrimination and the law

It is against the law for an employer or a would be employer to advertise a job that in any way discriminates against race or sex. After taking on an employee, the anti discrimination laws still apply to all other parts of the employees job, including wages and holidays.

Trade Unions

Make sure that you know about the various laws which safeguard your employees rights to choose whether to join a trade union.

Tax and National Insurance

Once you regularly employ people, you are responsible for deducting their income tax and National Insurance Contributions, and paying your own employers NI contributions. When you take on someone, you need to tell your local tax office. You will be sent documents which will show you how much you need to take out of each employees wages, and where to send the money. You must record each employees earnings and tax and National Insurance Contributions, and tell your local tax office about these amounts each year

In the case of National Insurance, The contributions for your employees will be in two parts. You must pay one part and your employee will pay the other. These contributions depend on how much you pay your employee. The Inland Revenue will collect them at the same time as

31

they collect any tax. Your local contributions agency office will be able to give you more advice on National Insurance.

Your personal insurance depends on your circumstances. If you are a company director, you will be treated in a similar way to your employees. You will be classed as an employee of your company and will pay contributions in the same way as your employees. However, there is no special way to assess directors National Insurance. You should contact the Contributions Agency Office for advice on this matter. If you are a sole trader, or partner, your contributions will be charged at the same rate each week. You must pay them every month by direct debit or every three months when you receive a bill. You may also have to pay an extra contribution for any profits your company makes. This is assessed and collected along with Income tax. You should tell the contributions agency office as soon as you become self employed.

The law and you as an employer

Having considered some of the main issues involved in employing people, you may want to become more acquainted with the following issues and how the law deals with them:

* terms of employment

* redundancy

32

* insolvency

* pregnancy

* suspension on medical grounds

* sick leave

* health and safety

* union membership

* itemised pay statements

* continuous employment

* time off for public duties

* unfair dismissal

* rights on ending employment

* union secret ballots

* limit on payment

* race discrimination

* sex discrimination

* equal pay

* disabled workers

* picketing

Although all of the above areas may not affect you, particularly in the early stages of development, if you do intend to employ staff then you should at least acquaint yourself with the areas.

Recruiting and motivating employees

Doing it yourself

You can do your own recruiting by advertising locally or in special papers. Or you could write to colleges and schools for candidates.

Job centres and employment agencies

The Job Centre, the Job Club, or the local careers office are all in business to fit people to jobs. Job Centres or careers offices give their services for free, but an employment agency could cost you as much as 20% of the employees first years salary.

Training

Training is necessary to make sure that staff know why and how a job has to be done. It can also help make them more efficient and help increase their productivity. Investing wisely in staff training pays off in the long run.

The personal approach

The better you treat your employees, the better they will treat you. If you are well mannered, punctual and committed they will be too.

Show them that they are valued, encourage their interest in the business and ask them for suggestions. They will probably respond positively but don't be patronising. You should ensure that you talk to employees, not down to them.

Have confidence in your workforce and allow them to get on with the job. Checking everything they do creates resentment and not much else. All good managers are able to delegate. Good delegation is really what management is all about.

You could also set targets and give bonuses. This way, you will encourage your employees to work harder. As a result you will increase productivity and waste less time.

35

Show appreciation-praise for a job well done is a real incentive. But try not to be over friendly. This is difficult when you are working one to one, but it might reduce your authority and it will be difficult to take a firm line if you ever need to.

In the next Chapter, we will move forward a step and consider marketing and also pricing a product. This is perhaps one of the most important areas of business and one which often receives the least attention.

5 THE MARKETPLACE

The next step in developing your business is to look at sales, which in turn means looking at the market and considering the most appropriate form of market research. Sales are vital to any business. Whatever you produce, you must be able to sell. This is necessary in order to survive.

You must be satisfied that there is a demand for your proposed business and you must be able to determine how you can investigate the market in which you want to operate, how many potential clients there are in either the catchment area you operate in or the wider area. If you work in publishing for example then clearly the market for your product would be different for that of a baker or butcher or plumber. A lot of thought needs to be given to this area.

Market Research

The tool that is used to determine demand for a product is market research. Market research can be cheap and simple or highly complex depending on how you approach it and what you might want to find out.

Market research, or effective market research should be able to provide you with information as to what people want and also how much they want and what they will pay for it. Competition which might exist should also come to light.

You should not be put off by competition nor should you believe that because there appears to be no local supplier that what you produce will sell. No supplier may mean no demand and competition may mean established demand.

The concept behind all market research is simple-the practice is often not and unless you have a lot of money the costs may be prohibitive. A good example might be a supermarket.

A potential supermarket would want to know concrete facts in order to establish demand. For example, in terms of the percentage of the population, the average number of visits made to a supermarket each year. This they may well be able to establish from their own records if they are part of a chain.

Secondly they would want to know, what distance people are prepared to travel in order to visit a supermarket. This will vary a lot but they would be interested in establishing a national average.

With these two facts the supermarket can then establish the catchment area population for the proposed supermarket. Now they need to know something about the competition. How many supermarkets are there in the catchment zone which might have an effect on the proposed supermarket? This is easily established. However, more difficult to determine is the effect on your potential business. If we suppose that the supermarket decides that only 30% of the catchment area is exposed to competition and that they expect that 50% of that 30%

38

would continue to use the supermarkets they presently use. This would mean an adjustment to predicted customer base.

However, competition comes from other shops not just supermarkets This is why calculations are based on average figures since this additional competition will be fairly standard throughout the country. A survey will be carried out in the locality to check that there are no special factors to consider-special factors which may cause adjustments to the predicted customer base either way.

The next question to be considered is; what is the average spend per visit per customer? Supermarkets will almost certainly be able to answer that one from existing records. From this data, they can predict gross sales and so the net operating profit. If this is not high enough to justify the expenditure, they might be reluctant to proceed with siting a supermarket.

The above is a simple model and does not take into account a number of complications but it does give an idea of how market research is carried out. There are two very important factors to be considered-average conditions in the industry and catchment area population, or a knowledge of that population. Although the example given covers selling to the general public the same principle applies when considering selling to other business.

It may be possible to determine industry averages by approaching trade associations. A visit to the bank is also very worthwhile as most high

39

street banks keep statistics which they would be willing to make available. A further source of statistics might be a major supplier in an industry.

Somewhat easier is to determine the magnitude of the target market. Businesses generally fall into one or two categories: those where the customer comes to the business to place the order and those where the business goes to the customer to get the order.

In the first category, the size of your target market will be a percentage of the local population. The size of the population can be found by contacting the records office at your local authority. The percentage which applies to your proposed business will be far harder to determine. The classic method is simple-ask a large enough sample to provide an accurate picture. This is easier said than done. A great deal of research experience is necessary in order to be able to design a questionnaire which can elicit all the right information.

If you can afford it, you could consider employing a market research agency to assist you. If you cannot afford it then you should spend time considering exactly what you want to ask and what you are trying to establish.

There are many other places which will hold the sort of information you might need. Your local training enterprise agency (TEC) or the trade association relevant to your business will be only too pleased to assist you.

Once you have established your target market, you might wish to consider exactly how you sell to that market. Easy if you have a shop in the middle of a busy shopping area, at least easier than if you produce books and have to cast your net far wider. It might be useful at this stage to look at marketing in a little more depth.

Marketing

You have carried out some form of research and now you are in a position where you wish to bring to peoples attention your product. Obviously different media are more suited to some businesses than others.

Marketing covers a whole range of activities designed to "identify, anticipate, and satisfy customer needs at a profit" (Chartered Institute of Marketing).

Three questions need to be looked at:

* When do customers want their needs satisfying?

* How do the customers want the need fulfilled?

* How much are the customers prepared to pay for that fulfilment?

41

Having found the answers to those questions we have to decide how best to communicate to the target market our ability to meet their needs at a price that they can afford-and communicate that ability to them at a price that we can afford. There are various options that we can consider. However, some of these options are expensive and may well not be within our reach.

Advertising

Advertising takes various forms. It is exceedingly difficult, unless you have deep pockets, to try to deduce the real effectiveness of whichever form of advertising you decide to employ. For example, is it cost effective to spend £800 on a small advert in a tabloid for one day if that £800 could be spent on something longer lasting?

Advertising hoardings and posters are one way. These tend to cover not only billboards but also tubes trains and buses. Hoardings are seen repeatedly by a wide and ever changing audience in the locality of your choice. They are usually inexpensive.

Leaflets

Leaflets can be distributed on a door to door basis (either to other businesses or to individual residences) or they can be given to individuals in the street. However, leaflets can also be thrown away as many see them as junk mail. The result is that leaflets tend to have a low strike rate. Leaflets can also be delivered as inserts in magazines

42

and newspapers. Magazines direct leaflets to specific audiences and newspapers to local areas. Both can prove expensive and again will be discarded more often than not.

A more effective use of leaflets is to have them available in places where the target market will see them. The classic case here is for businesses offering non residential facilities for holiday makers. These can usually be found in hotels and guest houses.

Another use of the leaflet is that of a poster in a newsagent or on other notice boards. This can be effective when being used to attract a defined group of the population who gather together in one place where leaflets cannot be made available. Universities or schools might be a good example.

Directories

Directories will fall into two categories-local and trade. Local directories such as yellow pages are well known mediums of advertising and they are reasonably priced, sometimes free. However, the effectiveness of such advertising depends on what you are doing and also where the ads are placed. Some businesses tend towards directories such as Thompsons because they have less advertisers and are cheaper.

Trade directories are different by their nature. They are unlikely to benefit new businesses as they can be expensive and are in some cases, nationally distributed. This is of little use if your business is local, of more use if your product is distributed nationally. There are now a number of local area and regional directories, often produced by trade associations . Some are available as a book or on disc for use with computers. Those who subscribe to the disc system often receive monthly or quarterly updates.

Advertising in magazines

Magazines fall into three categories-general national, local or specialist. Magazines tend to be more expensive to advertise in than newspapers but can be more effective. Magazines have a longer life expectancy than newspapers and are often passed on to other readers. Specialist magazines are read by specific people who may form part of your desired target audiences. It is worthwhile bearing in mind that most magazine are national.

Newspaper advertising

National newspapers can obviously reach a lot of people but also tend to be expensive. They are also of little value to those offering local services. Local newspaper advertising can be more effective and also cheaper. Free newspapers are cheaper but can be less effective as they also tend to be seen as junk mail.

Television advertising

It is highly unlikely that television advertising will be relevant in the early years of a business. To launch a television advertising campaign is very expensive indeed. Therefore, this medium will only be a consideration later on, if at all.

Radio advertising

This form of advertising would only be effective if there are sufficient numbers of listeners in the target market. However, in the right circumstances it can be useful and relatively inexpensive. Timing is very important in this medium as you need to target your slots at the most appropriate times and on the most appropriate programme for your intended target audience.

Using an advertising agent

Whether or not an advertising agency is employed will be a matter for the individual business concerned. This decision is down to cost. All businesses placing advertising should set an advertising budget. It could be that placing part of your budget with an agent proves far more cost effective than designing your own campaign. Agents are usually good at designing and placing adverts and can negotiate discounts with various media. It is certainly worthwhile consulting an agent in order to get an idea of what they can do for you, at the same time raising your own awareness of the direction you should be taking.

45

Direct mail

Direct mail falls into two categories: untargeted or blanket mailing or targeted. Targeted mail is usually far more effective as untargeted mail can be very expensive and also wasteful. Existing customers of a business are well defined and easily targeted. The secret with direct mail is to keep it short, simple and do it as often as is necessary.

Using sales representatives or agents

Whether or not you choose to use representatives or agents will depend on a number of factors. Where there are few sales required and the selling of a good is complex there may be the need for a representative. Where the product is simple and can be described in an advertisement or leaflet it is unlikely to be necessary to use a representative. There are two main types of representation, the representative or agent.

The representative is a paid member of staff who may or may not receive a bonus or commission based on results. All the representatives running costs will be borne by the business. An agent is a freelance who meets his or her own costs and is paid only on results.

The advantage of using the representative is that he or she uses their entire time devoted to your business and is under your total control.

46

The agent costs little to run. However, he or she is not totally dedicated to your business. If other products are easier to sell he may ignore yours altogether.

As you can see, there are a number of ways to reach your target audience, once that target audience has been defined. A lot of thought needs to be given to market research and marketing. All too often, they are the first areas to go through the window in search of savings or simply because you are too busy. However, well defined marketing can produce corresponding increase in profits and a clear strategy is an essential part of any plan when setting up a business.

Pricing Your Product

A well thought out pricing plan is essential to the future prosperity of your business, and will also help you to make the most of your opportunities.

To develop the right pricing plan for your business, you need to start by working out what your costs are. You need to look at what your competitors are charging and try to estimate what your service or product is worth to your customers. By knowing what costs you are incurring, you will be able to work out what your "break even" point is. How much do you need to sell before your business covers all its costs, including your own (essential) drawings, but before it makes a profit. Unless you can identify what your break even point is, you could operate at a loss, without realising until it is too late.

47

Your Costs

Costs can be divided into fixed (overheads) and variable (direct) costs. Fixed costs include your essential personal expenses, such as Mortgage, food etc, as well as rent, heating and lighting wages and interest charges. They tend to stay the same no matter how much you sell. Variable costs, however, increase or decrease according to your level of sales.

The most obvious cost here is the actual cost of materials required to manufacture the product but can include other things such as transport, postage or additional labour. The price you charge for your product has to cover all of the variable costs and contribute towards your overheads.

Outlined below is an example of a break even point.

Fred Peters Car Wash Ltd

	Cost per Annum
Personal Drawings	£10,000
National Insurance	£294
Tax	£500
Stationary	£100

Advertising	£400
Telephone	£320
Depreciation of Van (over 5 years)	£1,000
Petrol	£900
Servicing	£300
Road Tax Fund	£130
Insurance	£320
Business Insurance	£140
Materials	£200
Depreciation of Equipment	£200
Bank Loan £3,000 @ 12%	£200
Bank Charges	£100
Accountants Fees	£300
TOTAL	£15,404

Freds essential personal drawings to cover his family expenses is £10,000. He operates a small car wash. He expects to work for 46 weeks a year, allowing for holidays, sickness etc. He estimates that he will work 46 weeks a year, 38 hours per week.

His annual output is therefore:

46 weeks a year Times 38 hours times 0.5 cars per hour = 874

His break even point is

15,404

874

= £17.62 per car

After researching the market in his area, Fred believes he can confidently charge £20 per car, which will give him a reasonable profit.

Competitors Prices

Unless your service or product is much better than others on the market, you would be unwise to charge a price which is too far above your competitors, as you will find sales very hard too achieve. On the other hand, a low price often implies low quality or low standards.

Competing on price alone is a poor option. It is especially important for small businesses to differentiate themselves by other means, such as personal service, convenience or special skills. Customers rarely buy on price alone and it is worth remembering that you can more easily reduce your prices than put them up.

If, when you work out what your prices should be, they do not cover your costs-look again at how you might make your business viable. For example, could you reduce any of your variable costs, could you get supplies more cheaply, can you negotiate a discount or find an alternative supplier? On your fixed costs, could you trim any other expenditure?

Think again about what you are offering. Could it be improved and sold at a higher price? Can you sell different products for more money to increase your profits? Would sales increase if you put up your prices and spent the extra income on advertising and promotion?

Every cost incurred in running your business must be recovered either by what you charge for your time, or by the amount you charge for your products. Profits will be made only after all of your costs have been covered. But you may decide to use different prices in different situations. For example, a plumber offering a 24 hour service might decide to charge a premium rate for his services if he is called out during the night to deal with an emergency, a different rate for weekends and another rate for normal working hours.

51

Achieving a range of prices for the variety of skills offered, taking into account the time you would be likely to spend on each job and the convenience factor for your customers, can give you the flexibility to stay competitive, yet still provide a satisfactory income.

Hidden Costs and VAT

In addition to marking up the direct cost of what it costs to buy in goods and then sell them on, or to make a product and sell it, there are "hidden costs" which should be taken into account including stock and materials. Depreciation should also be allowed for. This is the amount set aside to spread the cost of equipment, machinery, vehicles and other assets over their useful lives.

Value Added Tax (VAT) is a tax on the value added to goods and services (Currently 17.5%) As such you will need to consider the impact this tax will have on the prices you set for your services or products. If the sales are above the annual threshold (check with your local VAT office) you are required to register for VAT. Leaflets explaining VAT and the laws surrounding it can be obtained from your local VAT office. In addition, there is a section in Chapter 6 concerning accounting for VAT.

6 RAISING FINANCE

Planning initial finance is crucial for the future success of a business. Most people who enter into business are not accountants and therefore do not have the knowledge or experience necessary to decide on the most appropriate way to finance their business. This is one area where people most often make mistakes because they are over optimistic about the amount of money they will make or have misjudged their cashflow situation.

Core Capital

You should remember that a fair amount of money is permanently tied up in the business as working capital, represented by stocks and debtors (less creditors). This is the core working capital and because it is virtually permanent it should be looked upon as part of the long term financial needs of the business. Never underestimate this.

There are three main ways of getting money: borrowing, investing or getting a grant.

Borrowing

Borrowed money is called loan capital and it eventually has to be paid back, usually with some interest added to it. The security may take the form of a charge on a specific business asset, or floating charge on all the assets which means that if your business fails the lender will get their money back before any other creditors.

If your business has no assets the lender will want some form of personal security from you, such as stocks and shares, an existing life insurance policy, a term life insurance policy, a charge on your home or a guarantee from someone else. If you decide to do this you will be putting your own security at risk. It is not something to be done unless you absolutely have to, because it removes the protection a limited liability structure would otherwise give you.

The usual course of action is to ask your bank manager for an overdraft. An overdraft is a temporary loan to tide you over between the time that you have to pay your suppliers bills and the time that your customers pay you. You will have to pay interest on this money, and the payments have to be made whether or not the business is doing well.

Borrowed money always carries a cost, so you need to find out about fixed and variable rates of interest. You should also ask the bank about arrangement fees, early repayment fees and non utilization fees.

For tax purposes, you can offset the interest on the loan or overdraft against profits, but this is not a good idea if it means putting your business in a vulnerable position.

Investing

You can invest in your own business or you can ask people to invest in your idea. You will need to speak to your accountant or solicitor if you intend to follow this path. Investment in your business should never mean loss of control or onerous terms in the future.

Getting a grant

Grants generally have to be applied for before you set up your business, though there are some exceptions. They normally have conditions attached to them. For more information about the range of grants available you should contact your local council or your local training and enterprise council.

Combinations

Most businesses combine the different types of finance, depending on their size. For example, you might decide to use any of the following combinations:

* Your capital and overdraft

* Your capital and overdraft plus bank loan

* Your capital and overdraft, bank loan and grant

55

* Your capital and overdraft plus bank loan and grant and investor

Look at the different types of money below and that should give you an even better idea of some of the options open to you.

Main types of finance arrangement

The most important thing to remember is to get the right type of money. Money is the life blood of any business and, without it, the business will die a quick and nasty death. It is vital to recognise that there are two types of business finance: borrowed short term money and medium/long term money. It is also very important to remember that businesses quite often fail if they don't get the right balance between owners money and borrowed money.

Short term money (up to three years) is intended to keep you going while you are getting paid, and to help buy raw materials. This is the working capital which is used to finance the current assets and its importance should never be underestimated. Examples are: bank overdrafts, short term bank loans, bills of exchange, debt factoring and invoice discounting, hire purchase and instalment credit and credit from suppliers.

Medium to long term money should be used to buy things that will last. This is called fixed capital and is needed to finance fixed assets (such as tools, buildings, equipment and vehicles). This money is tied up for three years or more. There are two types:

1. Where the aim of the business is to own the money, these are equity capital (ordinary shares and deferred ordinary shares) or preference share capital (preferred ordinary shares and preference shares).

2. Where the aim is to borrow money or get it from another source, You might choose any of the following medium or long term financial arrangements: mortgages; sale and leaseback of premises; hire purchase and instalment credit; lease; credit insurance and guarantee arrangements to help small exporters; project finance or joint venture finance; medium and long term bank loans; loan stocks and debentures; and convertible loan stocks.

Short term finance

Bank overdrafts

This is the most common form of borrowing. All you need to do is to talk to your local bank manager, though you will need to write out your business plan first (see Chapter 8). Interest rates vary, so don't make the mistake of borrowing a lot of money when rates are low and then be unable to pay them when rates increase. Banks charge for arranging overdrafts, so it is important to try to get it right the first time.

Term loans (short, medium and long)

This is a safer way of borrowing money, although it is more expensive than an overdraft and will involve the payment of fees. Term loans are used to meet your permanent working capital and can be taken out for periods of up to 20 years. They must either be secured against a fixed asset or personally guaranteed by you or another director.

Bills of exchange

very often a business can have customers but not enough money to finance producing its next order because of unpaid invoices. A bill of exchange is rather like a post dated cheque which is sold to a third party for cash. It can be used to supplement or replace overdraft facilities.

Debt factoring and invoice discounting

Customers who take a very long time to pay are a problem for business that is growing fast - and where cash flow is a problem. This problem can be solved by debt factoring and invoice discounting. This involves selling your trade debts to a company who will, in turn, charge you a fee. This service will cost you a little more than normal bank overdraft rates and you will need to be reasonably well established with a turnover of more than £25,000 a year (minimum). You can contact such companies through your accountant.

Unlike debt factoring, where all your unpaid bills are sold to the factor, in invoice discounting you need only to sell selected invoices. If your debtors do not pay the invoices you have sold then you will have to pay the money back to the discount house.

Hire purchase and Instalment credit

You may decide that instead of raising money to make an outright purchase you might wish to buy on lease or hire purchase terms. Again you should investigate charges arising from this method.

Trade credit from suppliers

Most companies use credit from suppliers to help finance their short term business. This credit can be negotiated (the usual terms range from 30-90 days) and should be weighed up against the cost of losing any cash discount. Remember to weigh the cost of the discount against borrowing the sum on your overdraft. Large companies tend to use this method as a means of securing non negotiated credit from smaller companies who have to pay interest on their loans and who can go bust while they are waiting to get paid.

Medium and long term money

Many people, when they first start their own businesses, dislike the idea of raising money from strangers. They feel that it will lead to loss of control. However, you can arrange the issue of shares so that you do not give individuals or a group of people control over your business.

There are different types of shares - the main ones are:

Ordinary shares

Deferred ordinary shares

Preferred ordinary shares

Preference shares

Ordinary shares

Here each share carries one vote and give the owner the same proportion of the assets and profits as every other share. These ordinary shares are risk capital and the owners of ordinary shares will lose their money if the business fails and get the full rewards if it succeeds. If the company is wound up owners of ordinary shares get nothing until other debts have been paid, including those of preference shareholders. A company can issue different voting rights. It is possible to keep more than 50% of the votes and not own 50% of the shares.

Ordinary shares are looked upon as permanent capital - they do not have to be repaid. However, a special "redeemable ordinary share can be issued - this means that it can be repaid at a later date and the owner of the business has the chance of regaining full control of his business at a later date.

Deferred ordinary shares

Although these are similar to ordinary shares the owners are not entitled to the dividends until the companies profits reach a certain level which then allows them to be paid. They may possibly not be allowed to vote.

Preferred ordinary shares

These give a minimum dividend even before a company pays a dividend on its ordinary shares. They will also probably have full voting rights.

Preference shares

Preference shares are not equity although they are part of the companies own money. They pay a fixed return out of the taxed profits. This money must be paid before any dividend on the ordinary shares. Preference shares can be redeemable - this means that they can be

repaid at a fixed future date. They can also be convertible - i.e. converted into ordinary shares later on. Another type of preference share is the participating preference share - these shares can

61

participate in the growth of the company once the profits have grown above a certain level. Until this point is reached they are entitled to a minimum fixed dividend. Unless the preference dividend has not been paid, preference shareholders are not entitled to a vote in the companies affairs or to attend company meetings.

Mortgages

Raising money on a property is a traditional way of providing business finance, and a mortgage loan from a bank or building society can give you medium to long term money at quite a reasonable cost.

Sale and leaseback of premises

Another possibility is leaseback. Here you sell the property then rent it from the company that purchases it.

Lease

When you take out a lease you rent the equipment from another company. Although you make regular payments on the equipment it will never belong to you.

Your decision to purchase or lease will affect your tax bill so it is important to speak to your accountant about this.

Credit Insurance and guarantee arrangements to help small exporters

There are special problems for businesses selling to overseas buyers, apart from the risk of fluctuating exchange rates. Overseas customers may be used to different credit terms and expect to be given longer in which to pay. It is often harder to check up on their reputations and harder to get paid. You can insure against these risks with a government agency called the Exports Credit Guarantee department (see Useful addresses) or a private credit insurance company.

Project finance or joint venture finance

In this type of finance arrangement, investors provide money for a project and then get a return on their investment consisting of a percentage payment on sales. Your accountant should be able to help you find such investors.

Medium and long term bank loans

These are uses to meet permanent working capital needs and can be take out to cover periods of up to 20 years. They must either be secured against a fixed asset or personally guaranteed by you or another director.

Loan stocks and debentures

Loan stocks are better for larger companies. Unlike a normal loan or overdraft, where you pay the money back to the bank, this kind of debt can be sold to other investors who in turn can sell it to other people. When the interest is due it will be paid to the person who finally owns the debt.

A debenture is similar to a loan stock, except that it is secured either on a fixed asset or as a floating charge. Should anything go wrong with the company, the owner of the debenture will be paid before any of the other creditors.

Convertible loan stocks

These are similar to loan stocks, except that the investor will have an option to change all or part of the loan into shares within the company.

How to approach lenders

Lenders are concerned about two things - getting regular interest payments and getting their money back. They will want security for the loan and if your business gets into trouble they will be repaid from the money you mange to get by selling these assets. They will also need to be convinced that you have the skills necessary to make your ideas work.

Before approaching anyone for money, you must be clear about your plans. You are far more likely to succeed if you can back up your idea with facts and figures. Look at the business plan in Chapter 8. Your accountant should also be able to help you with your business plan.

7 FINANCIAL CONTROL

In this chapter, we will consider the importance of financial control within the process of business planning. In particular, we will look at profit and loss forecasting, cashflow forecasting, effective book keeping and tax and insurance.

Profit and loss forecasting

A profit and loss forecast is a projection of what sales you think you will achieve, what costs you will incur in achieving those sales and what profit you will earn.

Having this information down on paper means that you will be able to refer to it, and adjust it as your business develops.

Cashflow forecasting

A cashflow forecast, as the name suggests, forecasts the changes in the cash which comes into and out of your bank account each month. For example, your customers may pay you after one month, whereas you might pay out for rent or insurance in advance. At the same time, you will have to pay for certain costs such as materials or wages and will need to budget for this.

Preparing a Profit and Loss Forecast

The example opposite shows you the range of headings which typically apply to many small businesses. Some headings may not be relevant to your business, but the example should help you to get an idea of how to prepare a profit and loss forecast. Many business support agencies and banks will help you to prepare a forecast.

Remember, a profit and loss forecast is a projection of what sales you think you will achieve, the costs you will incur in achieving those sales, and consequently what profit you will earn. As such, it represents a vital part of your overall plan for a business, as it shows you whether or not your plan is financially viable.

Notes to the profit and loss forecast

Sales is the value of work invoiced whether payment is actually received at the time or not.

Cost of materials is the direct cost of what you sell. If you are a retailer, it will be the cost of your stock; for an electrician, the cost of cable, flex etc. It does not include larger one off purchases.
Nor does the cost of these appear elsewhere in the profit and loss forecast. This is because they are regarded as part of your business assets.

PROFIT & LOSS FORECAST

Name of Business: WHITE BROTHERS PRINTERS
Period Covered: April '96 to March '97

*	Month APRIL		Month MAY	
	Budget	Actual	Budget	Actual
Sales (Net of VAT) (a)	12300	1475	12000	8480
Less: Direct Costs				
Cost of Materials	7900	7034	7700	5928
Wages	1000	882	1000	889
Gross Profit (b)	3400	3559	3300	1663
Gross Profit Margin (b/a x 100%)	27.6	31.0	27.5	19.6
Overheads				
Salaries	500	230	700	245
Rent/Rates/Water	100	100	100	100
Insurance	50	79	50	79
Repairs/Renewals	300	256	400	145
Heat/Light/Power	50	70	50	70
Postage/Printing/Stationery		50		
Motor & Travel				24
Telephone	200	271	200	254
Professional fees			500	500
Interest Charges	10	13	10	11
Bank Charges	50	106	50	274
Other	240		140	42
Total Overheads (c)	1500	1175	2200	1744
Trading Profit (b)-(c)	1900	2384	1100	(81)
Less Depreciation	100	73	100	73
Net Profit Before Tax	1800	2311	1000	(154)
Cumulative Net Profit	1800	2311	2800	2157

*These headings will, of course, vary according to your business.

OVERHEADS will vary according to the nature of your business. If you rent premises, for example, note the rent and other costs you are charged. If you work from home, calculate the additional costs of services (such as gas and electricity) you can attribute towards your business activity.

DEPRECIATION is a means of spreading the cost of equipment, machinery, vehicles and other assets over their useful lives.

VAT. For a VAT registered trader, VAT does not need to be included in the profit and loss forecast as it does not constitute a cost of the business. However, it should be included in your cashflow forecast.

Preparing a Cashflow Forecast

Remember that a cashflow forecast helps you to evaluate the timing of money coming into and going out of your business. In showing you the movement of money it takes full account of the fact that you may often not be paid immediately for work done and, correspondingly, that you may not have to pay immediately for goods and services you acquire. An important purpose of a cashflow forecast is to reveal the gap between your cash receipts and payments. It will show you whether or not, for example, you might need to borrow, and if so, when you are most likely to require additional funds. It is very common for businesses to need more cash as they grow because of the difference in timing of receipts and payments. See example opposite.

CASHFLOW FORECAST

Name of Business: WHITE BROTHERS PRINTERS
Period Covered: April '96 to March '97

*	Month APRIL		Month MAY	
Receipts	Budget	Actual	Budget	Actual
Cash Sales				
Cash from Debtors			14200	14980
Capital Introduced	5000	5000		
Total Receipts (a)	5000	5000	14200	14980
Payments				
Payments to Creditors	2200	2943	18320	12622
Salaries/Wages	1500	1112	1700	1134
Rent/Rates/Water				
Insurance	80	79	80	79
Repairs/Renewals				
Heat/Light/Power				
Postage/Printing/Stationery	20	50		
Motor & Travel				24
Telephone			200	271
Professional fees				
Capital Payments	1500	1498	1600	1586
Interest & Charges	100	119	100	285
Other				
VAT payable (refund)			2100	2060
Drawings			1000	800
Total Payments (b)	5400	5801	25100	18861
Net Cashflow (a-b)	(400)	(801)	(10900)	(3881)
Opening Bank Balance			(400)	(801)
Closing Bank Balance	(400)	(801)	(11300)	(4682)

*These headings will, of course, vary according to your business.

Notes to the Cashflow Forecast

Receipts is the money coming into your account, which will mainly be from your sales, but could be from other sources, such as money from a grant.

Payments is the money going out of your account, which will mainly be payments to your suppliers or creditors. The schedule of payments will vary according to the nature of your business. A cashflow forecast includes payments for capital items, such as a car or other vehicle used for your work and equipment, e.g., a computer and also drawings for other expenses.

VAT. All cashflow receipts and payments will be inclusive of VAT where applicable.

Other Terms

Working capital is the term often used to describe the short term resources used by the business for everyday trading purposes. This consists of:

* **Debtors**: these are customers you have sold to on credit, i.e. they owe you money.

* **Creditors**: credit, i.e. you owe them money.

* **Stock**: this represents the value of materials you have purchased. They may be purchased for immediate resale or they may be in the process of being converted into a finished article.

* **Cash**: this can either be the amount of physical cash you are holding or it may be money held in a current or bank deposit account.

All of the above have to be carefully controlled if your business is to prosper.

Overtrading

A problem common to many small and growing businesses is what is described as Overtrading. The more sales you make, the more money you will need to spend on funding material and debtors before you are paid for the sales. If your level of sales becomes too high and you do not have the necessary level of working capital to support it, you may simply run out of cash. This can be disastrous for your business and means that a full order book is not the only thing to strive for. Even with a profitable business and a full order book, it is imperative to have enough cash available. Extra finance can help your cashflow and make it easier to avoid the pitfalls of overtrading.

Collecting money on time

For every day a customer delays payments, your profit margin is eroded. You may have to pay interest charges on a loan or overdraft, when the money owed to you could be earning you interest instead.

Check your customers ability to pay

Before you offer customers credit, check that they can meet their liabilities. You may want to take up bank references.

Set out your terms of trading

Be specific about when you expect payment, for example, 30 days from the date of the invoice and make your customer aware in advance of work that you do.

Set up a system

Set up a system which enables you to issue invoices promptly and shows you when invoices become overdue.

Keep clear and accurate records

Inaccurate invoices or unclear records can be one of the main reasons for customers delaying payments. Make sure you send invoices punctually, to the right person at the right address.

Collect your payment on time

Establish a collections routine and stick to it. Keep records of all correspondence and conversations. Give priority to your larger accounts, but chase smaller amounts too. If regular chasing does not produce results consider stopping further supplies to the customer. If payment is not obtained, don't hesitate to ask a reputable debt collection agency or solicitor to collect the money for you.

Book Keeping

Spending money and receiving money is a constant process and each transaction must therefore be reduced to a monetary expression and then recorded in a Book of Account. The process of recording all this information relating to the financial affairs of the business is book-keeping.

The efficient management of the business will depend upon effective financial management, the key to which is to set up and maintain a simple method of financial record-keeping best suited to the particular business, one which is intelligible to your accountant and acceptable to the statutory authorities who also have an interest in the financial affairs of proprietors and businesses the Inland Revenue, the DSS and HM Customs & Excise.

Financial management means keeping track of all money coming in and going out, whether cash or cheque, where it comes from, where it goes to, how long it takes, what is being purchased and what is being sold.

For the individual planning to commence in business there must be a

Business Bank Account separate from the one in which personal money is handled.

Careful and regular scrutiny of the Business Bank Account Statements is a vital discipline, cross checking the books of account and the entries in them with those entries on the bank statements. You can make mistakes and so can your bank.

Every real transaction undertaken in the name of the business must be reflected by a financial transaction, evidenced by a financial piece of paper and entered in the books somewhere.

Consider though a cash transaction that does not generate a formal financial document such as an invoice or till receipt, for example a parking meter payment.

In such a case you must create your own piece of paper to back up your claim that a business expense has been incurred. Transactions of this kind are best handled by the use of Petty Cash. A petty cash voucher, showing the date, amount spent and what it was spent on is necessary evidence to satisfy your Accountant that a business expense has been incurred, not a personal one, and that you are entitled to charge it to the business.

The Books to Keep

There are basically four methods of book-keeping. Which one to choose will depend largely on the type and size of business you have established. Take advice from a business adviser or accountant if you are unsure as to which is the best one for your needs.

a) Proprietary systems.

These are best suited for sole traders in cash transaction types of business e.g. jobbing builders, market traders or some small shopkeepers. This type of business requires daily record keeping, often including till-rolls for the cash till and offers a simple method of control over finances.

A number of pre-printed stationery systems are available at business bookshops. Select one that allows you enough space to record all that needs recording. Worked examples are set out at the beginning of each book to show you how to keep cash records and the bank position, which can be calculated by following the instructions included.

b) The Analysed Cash Book System.

This is perhaps the most common method used by small businesses selling mostly on credit, with perhaps some cash sales. It relies on the Single Entry system of book-keeping, where each entry is, as the name implies, made once only, and all entries are made in one book, the Cashbook. The analysed cashbook is the bible of the business. It allows at a glance analysis because it is arranged on a columnar basis, showing how much has been received into the business, when and

76

from where, how much of each receipt is attributable to VAT and therefore how much is the net amount belonging to the business. All this information is written up on one side of a pre-printed book, the left-hand page, showing all monies paid into the bank on behalf of the business.

c) The Double Entry System

This method of recording accounts relies on ledgers, or separate books of account for each type of transaction. Far greater detail and control are possible using this system. As well as a cash account there is scope for setting up other ledgers such as the bought ledger for purchases, sales ledger, nominal (or business expense) ledger, salaries and so on.

It is much easier to monitor how much has been spent over a period of time on each type of transaction, simply by referring to the particular ledger or account, on each of which a running balance is struck. Every transaction is recorded in the major account called the Cash Account and also in the appropriate subsidiary ledger. In this way the Cash Account acts as a control account for all the separate accounts of the business. The most important feature of this system is the characterisation of all book-keeping entries as either a credit (he trusts i.e. the business owes him) or debit (he owes). The sophistication of this method lies in the use of two entries for each transaction.

For each credit entry in the Cash Account there must be a

corresponding debit entry for the same amount in a different account. Likewise for each debit entry in the Cash Account there must be a corresponding credit entry in a different account. The key words are Equal and opposite. That way the greatest possible degree of control is obtained.

d) Computerised Accounting Systems

A wide variety of off-the-shelf packages are available, which rely on single or double entry methods. It may be tempting to invest in an accounts package at the outset, especially if you intend to use other computer packages in the business. It would be most unwise to start using such a package without understanding the principles that underlie them. Businesses have failed because of the familiar GIGO (garbage in, garbage out). Money is the lifeblood of the business so don't turn it into garbage by neglecting an understanding of the what, why and how of book-keeping.

Accounting for VAT

A fully comprehensive guide to the complexities of the VAT system is beyond the scope of this book and only a brief outline will be provided. Suffice it to say that if you are registered for VAT with HM C&E then you are liable to account to that authority for VAT passing through your books. In effect you are an unpaid tax collector.

Your local VAT office will advise you on all VAT matters and enquiries

78

regarding VAT administration. Do not neglect to seek advice from C&E and/or your accountant before you commence business, because:

a) the best advice will depend upon the circumstances of your business; and

b) you will not be excused by HM Customs & Excise for failing to get advice. The C&E will presume you have been so advised on how the system works and what you have to do; and

c) the system is complex.

Registration

A) Compulsory registration

If you anticipate that the sales income of the business in the current trading year will reach the threshold level prescribed by law (contact your local VAT office). You must contact your local VAT office and inform them that the business is liable for registration for VAT.

Upon registration the business will be allotted a unique registration number, which must be shown on all business stationery.

VAT must then be charged on all sales the business makes, whether on credit or for cash, at the prescribed rate, except on those goods/services which are either zero rated or exempt. This is called the output tax.

The VAT paid by the business on purchases of materials etc. is called the Input tax.

HM C&E must be paid the amount of VAT charged by the business on sales (whether collected within the relevant quarter or not) minus the VAT paid by the business on its purchases. This is normally done at the end of each quarter, though a longer time period can sometimes be negotiated.

Retail businesses, i.e. those selling to the public, do not need to render VAT invoices unless a buyer requests one.

HM C&E publish a number of leaflets and notices explaining in great detail all you need to know about VAT and your business, as a sole trader, partnership or limited company.

Among the most important are:

i) VAT Notice 700: The VAT Guide. In fact a booklet of more than 140 pages.

ii) Should I register for VAT. This Guide is vital because HM C&E will impose financial penalties for failure to register when you should and also for late payments.

80

If you are fairly confident that within the next 30 days your taxable turnover for the past 12 months will exceed the threshold limit, then you must inform HM C&E.

iii) Filling in your VAT Return. A useful guide on what format to adopt and how to present VAT Return forms.

If you believe that you are not obliged to register, because turnover will remain below the threshold, you should still consider the issue carefully. There are circumstances when you can reclaim VAT incurred before registration, if you then register at a later date.

For example, VAT paid on vans (but not cars) and stock can later be reclaimed, disregarding the time of purchase, so long as the items are for business use. Of course you must produce VAT invoices to evidence the amount reclaimed.

If you engage the services of either solicitors or estate agents to set up the business, then VAT on their fee invoices can be reclaimed if they were incurred up to 6 months before the business was registered.

b) Voluntary registration

Compulsory registration arises simply because of the proximity of your turnover to the threshold level.

As an alternative you may want to consider voluntary registration, even if your turnover is substantially below the threshold level for compulsory registration.

The advantage is of course that Input tax paid on purchases subject to VAT can then be reclaimed.

The disadvantage is that VAT will have to be charged on the taxable supplies made by the business, which could well affect the competitiveness of your products/services. If competitors are not charging VAT and you are this might present a serious problem.

If the business is not registered, compulsorily or voluntarily, then it will have to bear the incidence of Input tax paid. You will have to consider whether the business can absorb this cost or whether you need to raise the selling prices.

8 PUTTING TOGETHER A BUSINESS PLAN

The following pages represent the basis for your business plan and the various sections relate to the sections of the book. If there are parts which you do not feel are relevant to your business, then you should ignore them.

You should construct your own business plan using the following as a guide. By referring to the book and also to the details of your own business you should be in a position to formulate your own plan which will be the complete document for your use, particularly for presentation to your bank manager or to other parties. Remember, it has been stressed throughout the book that an impressive business plan goes a long way towards developing your business and raising the necessary funds to go forward.

Your Business Plan

Name of business

_____

Address_____ _____

_____

Number_____
_____

Sole Trader_____ Partnership_____ Franchise___ Limited
Co_____

Start up date_____

Type of Business_____

Planning ahead

My ultimate goal is

_____

_____

I expect to achieve the following over the next few years

1_____

2_____

3_____

Marketing

I have identified my market
as_____
_____
_____
_____
_____
_____
_____
_____
_____

My customers may be described
as_____
_____
_____
_____
_____
_____
_____
_____
_____

Product comparison table

	My Product	Competitor A	Competitor B
Price			
Quality			
Availability			
Customers			
Staff Skills			
Reputation			
Advertising			
Delivery			
Location			
Special Offers			

After Sales Service

My product is special because

_____

_____

_____

_____

_____

_____

The main advantages of my product over my competitors are

_____

_____

_____

_____

_____

_____

Pricing

Calculating your break even point

Personal Drawings

_____

National Insurance

_____

Tax

_____

Stationary

_____

Advertising

_____

Telephone

_____

Rent and Rates

_____

Heating and Lighting

_____

Vehicle Depreciation

_____

Petrol

_____

Servicing

_____

88

Road Tax Fund

Insurance

Business Insurance

Bad Debts

Depreciation of equipment

Bank Loan

Bank Charges

Accountants Fees

Total Costs

_____

I intend to charge £_____ per hour/day/item

My break even point is

_____

Promotion and selling

My competitors promote and advertise themselves as following

_____
_____
_____
_____
_____
_____
_____

90

My promotion and advertising Intentions are

Method   Cost

_____

_____

_____   _____

_____

_____

_____

_____

I Believe these methods are appropriate for my market because

_____

_____

_____

_____

_____

_____

_____

Staying In Control

My sales projections are based on the following assumptions

_____

_____

_____

_____

_____

91

_____
_____
_____

The firm orders I already have are

Date	Order	Details	Delivery date
1_____		_____	_____
_____			
2_____		_____	_____
_____			
3_____		_____	_____
_____			
4_____		_____	_____
_____			
5_____		_____	_____
_____			

My current business assets are (e.g. equipment, machinery etc)

Item   Value   Life Expectancy

_____   _____
_____

_____   _____
_____

_____   _____
_____

_____   _____
_____

_____   _____
_____

I will need the following assets to start up and then throughout my first
business year

Start Up

_____

Item_____Value_____

Item_____Value____
_____

Year 1

_____

_____

Item_____Value__

_____

Item_____Value__

_____

The way I intend to pay for these are

Grants   Value   Date

_____

_____

_____

_____

Own Resources

_____

_____

Loans

_____

_____

Creditors

_____

_____

I can now obtain the following credit from my suppliers

Supplier   Estimate value   Number of
                                of monthly order   Days Credit

_____
_____
_____
_____
_____
_____
_____

Premises

My business will be located at

_____
_____
_____
_____

Because

_____
_____
_____

95

_____

_____

_____

Details of my lease/licence/rent/rate/next rent review

_____

_____

_____

_____

_____

_____

Details of key staff (if any

Name_____

_____

Position_____

_____

Address_____

_____

Age_____

Qualifications_____

_____

_____

Relevant work experience

_____

_____

_____

_____

_____

_____

P   r   e   s   e   n   t   i   n   c   o   m   e

_____

Repeat as necessary

I will need to buy in the following skills during the first two years

_____

_____

_____

_____

I estimate the cost of employing people or buying any services I may
need in the first two years

Number of people   Job Function   Monthly Cost   Annual cost

_____

_____

_____
_____

My personal Details

Name
_____

Address
_____
_____
_____
_____

T   e   l
(home)_____
_____

T   e   l
(work)_____

Qualifications_____
_____
_____
_____

_____

_____

D   a   t   e   o   f   B   i   r   t   h
_____

Business experience

_____
_____
_____
_____
_____

_____

Courses attended

_____
_____
_____
_____
_____

_____

Book-keeping

I intend to keep the following records
(which will be kept up to date by myself/book-keeper/accountant)

_____

_____

Other

Accountant

_____

_____

Address

_____

_____

Telephone_____

Solicitor

_____

_____

Address

_____

_____

_____

_____

_____

_____

Telephone_____

VAT registration number_____

Insurance Arrangements_____

Raising finance

By reference to my profit and loss and cashflow forecast, I need to borrow

Amount £

_____

_____

For

_____

_____

Period

_____

_____

I am investing £

_____
_____

_____

I can offer the following security

_____
_____
_____
_____

The above business plan will enable you to gain a clearer picture of your business and also give any potential funders an idea of whether or not you represent adequate security.

In the next Chapter, we will look at various methods of controlling your business, once it is up and running.

9 CONTROLLING YOUR BUSINESS

This Chapter builds on Chapter seven, Financial Control, concentrating more on day to day record keeping.

There are a number of common mistakes made by those who are in business, particularly people with very little experience. One vital mistake is allowing pressure to get in the way of formulating a longer term view of your business so that you can keep control of the future direction. Common mistakes are:

* Neglecting to make sure that you have enough stock.

* Getting too much new work and not finishing off existing work or not having enough money to pay for it.

* Not visiting new customers and quoting for work.

* Not being able to produce enough

* Not achieving high standards

* Charging too much or too little for your work.

* Forgetting to record orders and sending out invoices and statements.

* Not getting paid for all the work you have carried out.

Identification of key factors in controlling your business

When you first enter into business, your administration will probably be carried out at night or weekends. As soon as possible you should sit down and identify the key issues in terms of business control. All of the points mentioned above can be controlled if you have the right systems in place.

Putting systems in place to control your business

Once you have decided the key issues, you will then have to work out recording systems, so that you can analyze your results at the end of a given period, be it day, week or month.. Make the systems easy to use and get into the habit of using them right at the outset.

Office administration systems

Petty cash

Get some money from the bank and a petty cash voucher book and put this in a cash box. Keep a record of money spent and keep receipts.

Telephone

make sure your telephone is always manned during office hours and that you give the business name when you answer it. An answerphone should be installed if you cannot have someone there to take calls.

Recording orders

When you get an order from a customer, record it in a book straight away. Your record should include:

* Order Number

* Date of order

* Name of customer, phone number and delivery address

* Description of goods

* Quantity ordered

* Value of order

* Deliver date

This is very important, enabling you too see where you are at any given moment and that you do not lose business, or track of where you are with each job. In addition, you are providing proof of order and proof of delivery and final documentation to ensure that you can invoice for the work and get paid.

105

Filling In Job cards

For some businesses a job card for each customer will help you check how many hours are being worked. You should record the following information:

* Job number

* Name of person carrying out the work

* name of customer, address and phone number

* Customers instructions

* Order date

* Completion date

* Work carried out

* Number of hours worked

* Price charged

* Volume and cost of materials used

* Any other information about the customer you think will be useful to you in the future.

Preparing Invoices

As soon as you have finished an order you must prepare and send out your invoice immediately. Think about the information you should include on the invoice. Put the name and address of your business, name and address of your customer, VAT number if applicable, Date and invoice number, description of goods ordered and payment terms. You should have a pro-forma, or pre printed invoice which can be updated with the new number each time.

Sales Journal

When you send out the invoice you will need to record the customers name and other details. By recording this information you can keep track of how quickly your invoices are being paid and how long individual customers tend to take.

At the end of each month you should check the sales journal to see which invoices are unpaid. You must send a statement to each customer, listing all the invoices and the amounts that are outstanding.

Recording purchasing

In most businesses a lot of money is tied up in stock-in other words this money cannot be used as cash until the stock has been sold and paid for. Examples could be materials that still need to be processed and

finished products that need to be sold. The cost of keeping stock includes the purchase price, the interest on the money used to buy it, and the cost of warehousing or storage.

Stock control can be quite difficult and it is a matter of striking a balance between having what you need and not tying up money and space needlessly. This is where skilled analysis comes in and you need to really concentrate on your future production and sales before tying up money.

Purchase order forms

When you order stock, always keep a written note of what you have ordered and the terms and conditions you have specified, including delivery date. Always keep a record of the following:

* Purchase invoice number

* Supplier

* Total bill

* Precise requirements

* Order date

* Delivery date

* Payment terms

* Receipts (invoices)

Purchase Journal

This is similar to the sales journal but in it you write down the name of each supplier, the price and day when payment is due. You can also record what goods and services you have bought under different headings so that you can see what you have bought and when. This will give you a running check on your spending and an opportunity to check on your turnover, especially if you need to reduce your stock investment. Your purchase journal should record the following:

* Purchase invoice number

* Supplier

* Invoice date

* Total bill

* Date when payment is due

109

* Date paid

* Cheque number

Cash book

Your cash book will show two sets of information-money received and money paid out. You should be able to produce your monthly, quarterly and annual accounts from the information you have kept in your record books. See Chapter seven.

Remember, your business can only be controlled if you have control. It can only grow if you can use the information that is recorded in the systems that you have set up to assist you in future decision making. This is called business management and is every bit as important than the day to day hands on management that is essential to develop a new business. As the years roll by and your business grows, it may be that you will employ people to do your financial management. It may be that you do it yourself. However, it has to be done and in the initial phases it is very important indeed.

CONCLUSION

Throughout this book, I have stressed the importance of the key elements of business development, starting off with an idea through to developing that idea, marketing and pricing your product and controlling finances. Also, understanding the ideal structure for your business and having suitable premises to operate from. Keeping the books. Having a clear business plan to enable you to paint a broader picture of where you want to go. Finally, keeping control of the whole enterprise.

Of course, it is not expected that you become expert overnight. Some of the areas in this book may frighten you and make you realise just what hard work setting up and running a business is. However, it is hoped that by reading this book you will raise your awareness to the fundamental requirements of starting a business. If this has been achieved then you will stand every chance of succeeding in the future.

Don't be put off by the fact that at times it seems that you are spending a lot more than is coming in. All businesses suffer from this, whether old or new. large or small. It is easier to spend money than to make it. However, as a small business without much collateral, at times you may wish to give it all in and go back to the safety and security of a job.

Plan well, don't take unnecessary risks but don't be afraid to be bold. Keep control of all you are doing at all times. Know what you are doing in the early stages and where you are going.

Good Luck.

Useful Addresses

Advisory Conciliation and
Arbitration Service (ACAS)
Clifton House
83-117 Euston Road
London NW1 2RB

Tel 0171 369 5100

Association of British
Chambers of Commerce
7 Tufton Street
London SW1P 3QB

Tel 0171 222 1555

Association of Independent
Business
38 Bow Lane
London EC4M 9AY

Tel 0171 329 0219

BNR Business Names Registration
Somerset House
Temple Street
Birmingham B2 5DN
Tel 0121 643 0227

British Franchising Association
Franchise Chamber
Thames View
Newtown Road
Henley on Thames
Oxon RG9 1HG

Tel 01491 578049

British Overseas Trade Board
1-3 Victoria Street
London SW1E 6RB

Tel 0171 215 5000

British Technology Group
101 Newington Causeway
London SE1 6BU

Tel 0171 403 6666

Business in the Community
8 Stratton Street
Mayfair
London W1X 6AH

Tel 0171 629 1600

Business Links

See local phone books or
Small firms and business links
Division

Department of Trade and Industry
Level 2
St Marys House
Sheffield S1 4PQ

Tel 0114 259 7507

The Chartered Institute of
Patent Agents
Staple Inn Buildings
High Holborn
London WC1V 7PZ

Tel 0171 405 9450

Companies Registration Office
Companies House
Crown Way
Cardiff
CF4 3UZ

Tel 01222 388588

Confederation of British
Industry (CBI)
Centrepoint
103 New Oxford Street
London WC1A 1DU

Tel 0171 379 7400

Department of Social Security
Richmond House
79 Whitehall
London SW1A 2NS

Tel 0171 210 5983
Freephone 0800 666 555

Department of Trade and Industry
1-3 Victoria Street
London SW1E 6RB

Tel 215 5000

Department for Education and Employment
Moorfoot
Sheffield S1 4PQ

Tel 0114 275 3275

Forum for Private Business
Ruskin Chambers
Drury Lane
Knotsford
Cheshire WA16 6HA

Tel 01565 634467

Health and Safety Executive
Chancel House
Neasdon Lane
London NW10 2UD

Tel 0181 459 8855

International Association of
Book keepers
Burford House
44 London Road
Sevenoaks
Kent TN13 1AS

Tel 01732 458080

Local Investment Networking Agency (LINC)
4 Snow Hill
London EC1A 2BS

Tel: 0171 236 3000

National Federation of
Small Businesses
32 Orchard Road
Lytham St Annes
Lancashire FY8 1NY

Tel 01253 720911

Scottish Enterprise
120 Bothwell Street
Glasgow G2 7JP

Tel 0141 248 2700

Small Business Bureau Ltd
Curzon House
Church Road
Windlesham
Surrey GU20 6BH

Tel 01276 452010

Welsh Development Agency (WDA)
Pearl House
Greyfriars Rd
Cardiff CF1 3XX

English Enquiry 0345 775577
Welsh Enquiry 0345 775566

OTHER STRAIGHTFORWARD GUIDES

A Straightforward Guide to:

Computing

Private Tenants Rights

Teaching Your Child to Swim

Teaching Your Child to Read and Write

Small Claims in the County Court

Personal Finance

Book-keeping and Accounts for Small Business

Tiling For Beginners

Caring for a Disabled Child

Divorce and the Law

Leaseholders Rights

The Straightforward Business Plan

The Straightforward C.V.

If you would like Straightforward to Publish your book, please contact us at: 38 Cromwell Road, Walthamstow, London E17 9JN.